MY OXFORD

WINNER OF THE NEW WELSH WRITING AWARDS 2017

MEMOIR CATEGORY

My Oxford

Catherine Haines

New Welsh Rarebyte is the book imprint of New Welsh Review Ltd,
PO Box 170, Aberystwyth, Wales, SY23 1WZ,
www.newwelshreview.com, @newwelshreview,
Facebook.com/newelshreview
Copyright © Catherine Haines, 2019
ISBN: 978-1-9993527-2-1

The right of Catherine Haines to be identified as the author
of this work has been asserted in accordance with the
Copyright, Design and Patents Act, 1988.

A CIP record for this title is available from the British Library.
All rights reserved. No part of this publication may be reproduced,
stored in a retrieval system or transmitted at any time or by any means
electronic, mechanical, photocopying, recording or otherwise without
the prior permission of the copyright holder and publisher,
New Welsh Review Ltd.

Editor: Gwen Davies
Design & typesetting: Ingleby Davies Design
Cover image: Cristina Romero Palma/P G Amrt/Shutterstock.com

New Welsh Review Ltd works with the financial support of the
Welsh Books Council & Aberystwyth University

Dedicated, *in memoriam*, to Howard Mak (1987-2009)

...We are oft to blame in this

'tis too much proved, – that with devotion's visage,
and pious action we do sugar o'er
the devil himself.
> *William Shakespeare, Hamlet*

What follows is, in its essence if not in its contours, a memoir about my experience with anorexia nervosa while I was a postgraduate student at the University of Oxford. My intention is not to contribute to the plethora of 'treatment texts' written by 'recovered' anorectics. (I am not 'recovered': I am 'recovering'). I would like to impart some information, ideas, and feelings about some aspects of my experience to others currently suffering from an eating disorder, directly or indirectly. I've chosen to narrate and reflect on the year I spent in Oxford because I would like to a) question whether a possible equation exists between my compulsion to starve and pressure to read and write and b) re-consider the religious conversion I underwent during that time.

1. Hong Kong

At the beginning of July 2011, I went on a diet.

It was the summer between my bachelor degree and graduate school. I was staying with my parents in their apartment in Hong Kong. I had gained weight, and felt that the most effective use of time would be to focus on losing it. My mother suggested the Cambridge Weight Plan, a programme which is based on the concept of meal replacements, sachets of minerals and nutrients, which contain 200 calories each and dissolve in water. Combining three of them a day with a meal of pure protein supposedly provides a balanced diet.

Cambridge works partly by pushing the body into a state of ketosis. Ketosis is a Greek word meaning 'sweet condition', and accounts for the 'high' that anorexics routinely cite. It is the consequence of a diet that is very low in carbohydrates. A body denied sugar enters a metabolic state, during which it is almost completely fueled by fat. These release 'ketones' into the blood stream. Ketones are the most addictive compound on earth. Just as a heroin addict chases substance-induced highs, anorexics depend on chemicals – our own. Anorexia strikes classically good girls in good families. Good girls are often people pleasers and perfectionists but we, too, can become drug addicts.

There was a lot of pre-reading for my course, and I was writing a novel, so I established a routine to facilitate these practices while I was fasting. By the end of August I had accomplished my academic, creative and weight-loss goals. To this day, I do not know why I failed to resume my (abnormal, bulimic, disordered) relationship with food. I simply continued to do what I had already been doing: every day, I restricted my nutritional intake to 1,000 calories or less. This continued throughout the months I was completing my Master's degree, so that by July 2012, I was very severely underweight and had been diagnosed with anorexia nervosa.

2. Michaelmas

The St Peter's College MCR (Middle Common Room) refers to two things: firstly the group of postgraduates within the College and secondly, the common room itself in which we socialised and worked. It was here during Noughth week (the week before term starts) that someone asked me: 'What are you writing your dissertation on?'

'The mind-body problem.'

'I thought you were studying English?'

'I'm interested in the overlap between philosophy and literature.'

'What text will you study?'

'*Hamlet.*'

'Then you can tell everyone what "to be or not to be" actually means.'

'Exactly.'

'What *does* it mean?'

'Is it better to be alive or not alive? Or rather, is it better to exist or not exist?'

'Life isn't that bad.'

'Death might be worse. It all depends on whether or not you believe in the immortality of the soul.'

'He's debating whether or not to kill himself, right?'

'That is how it is traditionally understood."

"Why does he want to kill himself?'

'That is the question.'

'Ah hunh. It's a cool topic... I'm getting hungry. Shall we go to dinner in hall?'

'Is it time?'

'Just about.'

'I'll head off, then. I've got some stuff to do back in my room. See you later.'

I walked out the back gate of the college, through the Castle Complex, onto Paradise Street, into the St Peter's Graduate Annexe, up the stairs, opened my door, lay on the bed, and fainted.

The following day I met my supervisor for the first time. I explained that even though I had but a cursory understanding of analytical philosophy, and had never studied theology, I wanted to a) define and contextualise the sixteenth-century model of the self and b) explain Shakespeare's position with regard to it. My supervisor explained that in order to fully appreciate Shakespeare, I had to understand every thinker preceding him. He suggested I start with Plato and go as far as Luther via Augustine and Aquinas before beginning to analyse *Hamlet*. Try and fit that in by Christmas while learning two ancient languages, sleeping five hours a day and living on 1000 calories. As I left my supervisor's study and walked towards the Bodleian, I resolved to drop my BMI to eighteen by Easter, just to see if I could. It was a matter of pure curiosity.

Each day, I wake at precisely 4am. Strip, go to the bathroom, step onto the scales. Breath. Make a cup of herbal tea, sit at the desk and take notes until 6am. Walk down Paradise Street to the gym. Run for 60mins, burn 500 calories. Return to the Annexe, shower, exfoliate, moisturise, dress. 9am. Make an omelette – two eggs, 70 calories each, 140 calories, plus cheese, 60 calories, 200 calories. 800 calories remaining. Walk to the library. Study....

Plato's conception of the mind-body problem says that the soul, caught in the 'grave of the body', is liberated through a weakening of precisely this body. Salvation occurs when the soul is set free from its prison-body. The soul is then free to live in the realm of pure forms, where it 'can behold the absolute Good.'

A bit dizzy? A throat lozenge? Step outside for a cigarette. Lip gloss *and* chewing gum? 11:30, go to Pret a Manger. Buy 100 calories. Protein or green veg. Consume. 700 calories remaining. Return to the library. Study....

Plato's explanation impressed the hypersexual St Augustine of Hippo and the overweight Thomas Aquinas centuries later. In 1517, Luther also more-or-less agreed, saying, 'Man has a twofold nature, a spiritual one and a bodily one.'

2pm. Consume 200 calories. 500 calories remaining. Walk to class. Burn excess by walking fast. Speak. Listen. 4:30, go to Marks and Spencer and have another 100 calories. 400 calories remaining. Go to the MCR. Talk. Listen. Go back to the Annexe. Shower, change, email, go to dinner, at college or with friends. 400 calories of protein and greenery and alcohol included. 'End Game'. 10pm, go to bed. Sleep. And again.

For months, I closely studied medieval Christian thinkers, all of whom claimed that mind and matter are separate and ergo that the soul is a) immortal and b) damnable. By Easter I had lost so much weight that I had to wear four layers of clothes to stay warm. Dionysius was likewise driven mad by his education.

A growing body of research has focused on the relationship between the frequency with which women read and their potential anorexic risk. Mainly this work links the presence of eating-disordered thinking with women's reading of beauty and fashion magazines, rather than their reading of poetry and philosophy from Homer to Rousseau. But in any case, the notion of disordered reading suggests that certain subjects are inherently more open to being affected by text; that our boundaries are essentially more permeable, more receptive to the leaky toxicity of words. We are 'dupes' who consume too many unsound ideological representations.

3. Christmas and New Year

I spent the Christmas holidays with my extended family in Scotland. It was the ultimate nightmare. I hadn't been in a situation where I was 'required' to eat three meals a day for six months – I had certainly eaten no more than a single meal once or twice a week, in front of friends, for the duration of that time.

When I first arrived at my uncle's house, I tried to maintain my structured 'system' of 1,000 calories of pure protein a day, while appearing to eat 'normally'. Thus mealtimes brought tremendous stress, anxiety, and fear. I had to manage people and their perceptions in addition to my own willpower. Needless to say, everyone noticed and my eating habits were a hot topic of discussion, and so I ate more, in order to assuage their censure. Consequently, I experienced food as force. The guilt I felt when I 'overate' was enormous and I was desperate to find opportunities to make up for all the 'extra' calories I had consumed. I couldn't stop thinking about the food or tabulating what I'd eaten at the expense of enjoying myself and socialising. Just worrying about how to socially engineer the situation was exhausting.

For New Year's Eve, I travelled to Rome to celebrate with a friend from High School. This particular friend has seen me through every stage of my illness, by providing unconditional support and without expressing criticism. On that occasion, as she has on others, she succeeded in loosening me up. During our holiday, I ate gelato and drank champagne, I had pizza and pasta, and, at the time, I didn't feel guilty about it. That was the last time I ate by choice.

Our visit to the Vatican drove home for me the reality of a lot of the material I had been studying in theory and reading in isolation. My friend and I had a number of very serious religious discussions – she herself is a lapsed Catholic – as a result of which I actually considered Damnation for the first time in my life, and to accept damnation as a realistic possibility means to take on the hardest battle any human being can fight.

4. Hilary

When I returned to Oxford I had a conversation with a priest. I had been christened when I was a child, but I was deeply concerned about the state of my soul. I wanted to be confirmed and come into full communion with the Church. The priest said this would require a period of Catechumenate. He placed my name on the Rite of Election, and said that if he were convinced that I was ready to make a faith commitment to Jesus, I could receive the sacrament of the Holy Eucharist at Easter.

I observed Lent, which meant embracing my fast with a ferocity of newness, restricting further the amount and type of food I ate. Regarding it as the final period of purification and enlightenment, I promised myself – promised God – that I would begin to eat on Easter Sunday and enter the moment of Resurrection. I would be saved and my new life would begin.

I struggled to uphold my previous routine that term, because I was no longer able to eat even 1,000 calories, and the protein stuck in my throat. I had a violent, visceral reaction of nausea and repulsion – akin to an epileptic fit – whenever I saw food, and whenever I ate, I experienced extreme pain. Consequently, I felt always as though I were about to faint. The moment I began to carry on an extended conversation with anyone, even a shopkeeper or a librarian, I would see stars. I was unable to remember the start of my own sentences upon their completion. I could not hold several numbers, or several words, or several complex concepts simultaneously. I ceased connecting one thing to the next, ceased even feeling obliged to do so. I stayed in my room, wrapped up in blankets, in front of a blow heater, working with the text of *Hamlet* (Otherwise known as *Spectre Afoot!*).

Hamlet begins one night on the ramparts of Elsinore Castle, when Prince Hamlet encounters the ghost of his father, the late King. Prince Hamlet says:

> *Be thou a spirit of health or a goblin damned*
> *Bring with thee airs from heaven or blasts from hell*
> *Be thy intents wicked or charitable.*

He doesn't ask, 'Are you real or not?' There can be no question. There is a ghost. The Elizabethan audience knew it. The ghost was real in their belief system. We know it too. It's in the list of characters and is listed as a speaker in the text. (We also know it's an actor. That is, it is both real and not real) So when the ghost tells Hamlet that his father was murdered by his uncle, the current king, Claudius, and demands that Hamlet avenge him, Hamlet agrees to do as instructed. Privately, however, Hamlet, remains uncertain of the ghost's veracity.

I closed the book. It was dinnertime and I'd promised a friend I'd meet him at the Turf Tavern. So I got dressed, wrapped myself in my coat, and headed for the door, just as I'd done countless times before, when a voice observed, 'You are leaving the room.'

I looked around and there was no one there. I walked on, down the stairs, across the hall when she spoke again.

'You are opening the door,' she said.

I stopped, and closed my eyes. My head spun. I stepped outside.

'You are walking along the street.'

I saw stars. I was worried I would collapse so I walked back towards my room very slowly. I paused outside the kitchen. Perhaps if I ate something....

'Do Not Eat,' said the voice.

I lay on my bed and closed my eyes. I started replaying my own actions in my head while she commented on them. I had a sense of looking at myself through the critical eye of another, watching my own figure– my 'double' – viewing the scene from up above....

I woke up the next the morning and made an omelette for breakfast. As I lifted the fork to my mouth, the voice said, 'Do

Not Eat!' and my wrist flicked, throwing it against the wall.

Frightened that I had some sort of involuntary muscular disease, I went to the doctor.

'What seems to be troubling you?'

'I haven't had a period for six months.'

'Is there any possibility you could be pregnant?'

'No.'

'Have you experienced tiredness?'

'Yes.'

'Lie on the bed.' He pressed into the lower part of my stomach with his fingers. When I sat up again, he listened to my chest, and then asked me to get on the scales.

'Have you noticed any weight loss?' he asked.

'Yes, I suppose so.'

'It's possible you have Crohn's disease, which is a chronic bowel disorder. Alternatively, this is a hormonal imbalance. We should run some tests.'

'Alright,' I said, standing up to leave. He looked at me.

'Sit down again for a moment please,' he said. 'There is a chance... do you think you might have an eating disorder?'

'No,' I said.

'Are your thoughts or behaviors around food or weight

making it difficult for you to enjoy life?'

'No.'

'Alright. I'll book you in for an ultrasound. You can go now, go see the nurse for a blood test and urinary sample.'

I walked out the door and out of the clinic and never went back. It was extremely cold. I headed down Walton Street towards the Annexe. My hands were purple. I was lightheaded: there was a party that night, so I was saving all my calories to have in front of friends. I decided to rest until it was time to get ready.

There was a knock on the door.

'Yes?'

'Are you OK?'

'Um, yeah, fine.'

'You didn't show up tonight or last night, and you're not answering your phone. Can I come in?'

'Just give me a sec.'

I pulled on my dressing gown and opened the door.

'You look awful,' he said.

I saw myself reflected in the glass window behind him. I was skeletal. My shoulders were hunched and my eyes were hooded. I looked like a Devil.

'It's just the flu.'
'Can I get you anything?'
'No, I'm fine thanks.'
'Ok. Well, let me know if there is anything I can do….'
'I'll let you know.'
'Cath?'
'Yes?'
'Why don't you eat something?'

Most days, someone said, *why don't you eat,* as though I were making a choice to refuse food. Switching off hunger isn't purely volitional. What people don't understand is how scared I was, because I *couldn't eat.* I wanted to eat. I really did. But I genuinely believed that it was the wrong thing to do, and therefore that I would be punished if I did it. If I ate, I would go to Hell.

5. Easter

I sat alone on the far end of one of the pews, with the other Catechumens. After a series of scripture readings, we were presented to the parish community, who prayed for us with the Litany of the Saints. Next, the priest blessed the water. We renounced our sins and professed our faith, after which we were anointed, sealing the covenant created in baptism. Once all the Catechumens had been blessed, we were invited to take communion.

I knelt and bowed my head in humility and modesty while I took the bread and wine. It was an act of sacred cannibalism, in symbolic form, I was eating Jesus, becoming Jesus, the tasting was literal, I ate the end of shame, the end of guilt, I ate Grace. I understood quite literally that Christ died to save me – by providing bread I had earned during months of hunger hell.

I returned to my room. I had planned to break my fast with a hot cross bun, since not only is bread the body of Christ, but also I had not eaten carbohydrates for months. Folklore said that a piece of it was given to someone who was ill to help him or her recover. I went to my room and looked at the bun and picked it up and ground it into dust and placed it in the bin.

I was just about sensible and rational enough to know in body and mind I was ill, but I had so many restrictions and limitations in place, so many laws and so many precise habits. My System was ultimate, and challenging it would lead to Doom. I had no idea how to exit. I knew I had not reached the moment of return, but was only now beginning the process of descent. Steel cold fear gripped me and I felt I really might die.

6. Trinity

Most anorexic women wait mutely all their lives rather than profane the purity of a page with anything less than what is perfect. Texts I produced in the throes of the illness, such as my dissertation, *On Grace and Will*; *Swan Song*, the bildungsroman I wrote in 2012, and my diaries, are typically opaque, apparently schizophrenic: they contain pronouns, impersonal sentences, torrents of undigested quotations, which make a patchwork quilt, impenetrable as a *palimpsest* and confusing for the reader. I turned to a splintered or fragmented form of composition, and produced work more on the side of 'figuration' than 'representation'. Anorexic text is similar to the anorexic woman, in that it undertakes the torturous task of saying something without speaking.

Clarissa, or, the History of a Young Lady by Samuel Richardson, is regarded as the longest novel in the English language (*Hamlet* is the longest play). The heroine starves herself to death in penance for – or, perhaps, revenge against – her rape. The novel uses a strange excess of words in contrast to the savage reduction of Clarissa's flesh, as if the body of the starver is devoured by an internal verbosity. Words, strange and vampiric, feed on flesh. In recent decades, a prominent strain of Richardson criticism has been the argument that the erotics of the text undermine the author's expressed intention to provide a heroine who is morally exemplary. Some critics go so far as to suggest that Clarissa is complicit in her own rape.

How different, then, was it to be raped by a suitor in 1747 than today? Violent partners still depend on the complicity of the society around them and the silence of their victims, who fade into anorexic Christian martyrdom, as Clarissa does. I have nothing but admiration for the way Richardson depicts her efforts at recovery: centuries before talk therapy and trauma theory, Clarissa goes over the event again and again, in letters and in reported conversations, remembering, meditating, and praying over it, accounting for what she might blame herself for and what she suffered undeservingly.

Unlike other kinds of addictions, anorexia disguises itself as virtue. It felt good to deny my appetites and suppress my hungers, to excise them, or cause them to not be, which is another way of saying I had begun to feel that desire was inherently wrong. I felt it was bad to allow things to penetrate my body, and flesh was proof of having done so in the past, proof of my previous 'sins'. By denying my desires I was able to erase them, which was a way of conquering myself. I wanted to create a pure, empty and static inner space, free from contamination or intrusion. I felt that my body was 'sullied', and wished it would 'melt' (The first line of Hamlet's first soliloquy, 'O, that this too too solid flesh would melt' is hotly debated among editors and scholars. The First Folio reads 'solid,' but the early quartos read 'sallied', a variant of 'sullied.' I favour the later.)

In a book called *On Shakespeare and Christian Doctrine,* I had come across mystic and philosopher, Simone Weil. She says that 'at the centre of the human heart, is the longing for an absolute good' and to achieve this, she demands a continual 'self-erasure' and 'detachment' from the 'ego'. My path had in common with Weil's a 'self-effacement' or 'de-creation', to use her terms. I became fascinated by her perilous emphasis on self-renunciation, her struggle to formulate a 'rhetoric of faith' of terrifying severity: my greatest desire was to become self-less, 'to lose all personal being' which is the condition Weil says is necessary to experience and know 'truth'.

Eating disorders have inspired a perverse literary tradition – an *ecriture faminine* – replete with patron saints (Catherine of Siena, Simone Weil), glamorous elders (Emily Dickinson, Jean Rhys), tropes (fairies, snow), and devices (paradox, irony, the unreliable narrator). In 'How to Disappear Completely: On Modern Anorexia', Kelsey Osgood argues that 'the person writing about her own struggle fuels the fire by producing a long, hubristic poem, an elegy, an ode' to the illness. She thinks 'we make anorexia desirable by connecting it to brilliants and also by talking about it poetically, by making it something that enhances a person's aura, makes them more glamorous.' I do not agree. I think that by committing the self-mythologising qualities of their sickness to paper, 'recovering' anorectics are trying, in their way, to express an entire system of metaphysical belief.

In the depths of my illness, I didn't regard myself as a

fragile poet-fairy or believe I could paint with all the colours of the wind. I didn't imagine I could subsist on the minerals from the air, like an orchid. I looked death in the face, and by death, I mean death as we live it today, without God, without hope of salvation.

7. Hong Kong

Once I had submitted my dissertation – a minor miracle – I returned home to Hong Kong and, within a few weeks, my BMI had dropped again. I had begun to invent new ways to occupy my fanatic interest in numbers and orders and systems in order to 'prove' the existence of the soul. What follows is an example of the blatant nonsense, which composes my diary entries from that time:

$E=MC2$. 'c' is the speed of light, 'm' is the mass of anything, 'E' is the equivalent energy of that mass. This equation means that mass acts in accordance to the forces of light, to become energy, movement, action, 'life'. My mass is 46kg, but I'll round it to 50.

According to Einstein's equation, I am a bundle of energy equivalent to –

$$E = mc^2$$
$$= m \times c \times c$$
$$= 50 \text{ kg} \times 300000 \text{m/s}^2 \times 300000 \text{m/s}^2$$
$$= 4{,}500{,}000{,}000{,}000 \text{ Joules!!} \text{ That's } 1.07552581 \times 10^{12} \text{ calories!}$$

With this energy, I could supply electricity for the entire world for days! If the average man burned 2,000 calories a day, I have enough energy for 18416 human lives of 80 years each! The Buddhists were onto something! In a sense, I have more than one life. But human beings don't have enough technology to convert ourselves into pure energy.

If it were possible to convert matter fully into energy then I could calculate the total annual energy requirement of human kind. In 2005 the Earth's total energy use was 5×10^{20}J. $m = E/c^2$ so $m = 5 \times 10^{20} / 9 \times 10^{16} = 5500$kg – just 5.5 tonnes of matter. But matter cannot be converted into energy without the inclusion of light – 'c' – this backfires. It will not be removed from the life possessing it. Some people argue that it weighs 21g. Not so. Light, like 'qi' and spirit, is massless, but I nevertheless operate in accordance to it.

One day, when I was out running, I fainted.

I didn't 'See the Light'. I had the opposite experience.

I was teleported to Hell, where Harpies escorted me into a cell. I saw a group of young people within and blurted out, 'Oh, we must be the suicides!' but no matter how much I tried, I couldn't elicit a response from any of the damned souls around me. The cell had snakes all over the ground. They threw me against the walls and pierced my flesh with their claws. My flesh was eaten right to the bone, only to immediately grow back so they could eat it again.

Hell was not red and noisy. Hell was an absence of sense, there were no screams or sounds, Hell was not populated, it was only 'I' and the 'I' that thinks and not the Eye that sees. Burning there was, but it was not fire or ice burning or anything of flame or water, it was only self-burning, just a self, the self, burning for and on its self, fuelled on and by and for its self, self-consumed and so becoming less and less as it burns more and more inwards releasing the chemical composition of its heart into its bloodstream and evaporating it.

Three minutes later, I woke up.

That is my happy ending. I woke up.

Yes, Hamlet does appear as a Christ-figure in the final

scene, because he dies and through his suffering, the soul (of Denmark) is saved. The New Testament's story is not, to put it mildly; the only one humanity has ever come up with about a Dying God. Transcendent power goes down to the dark and allows itself to be extinguished but then returns all the stronger. Selves, like stars, are entitled to eclipse. You get the happy ending *because* of the tragic one.

The psychologist William James (1842–1910) draws a contrast between two different kinds of people, the 'once-born' and the 'twice-born'. He says that the twice-born war with their flesh and live one long drama, and that, in a desire to understand the meaning of life, this attitude inevitably leads to a psychopathic crisis. He says that the process of unification, while gradual, can and does occur, and it transforms the most intolerable misery into the profoundest and most enduring happiness. But that's another story.

Anorexia is not a trivial concern. Anorexia is a fatal disease that has the highest death rate of all psychiatric illnesses. It may be a gross misunderstanding of Neo-Platonism, or an unusually disastrous variant of Cartesian dualism, but anorexia is not just a relentless pursuit of thinness. What am I really? What is the substance that stands the change and is the actually existing thing? There is something more eschatological at stake in self-starvation than the fashionable taste for slenderness or the equally fashionable ideology of self-control. Striving to be thin conceals the ideal not to have a body, which is not a trivial concern. Anorexia is a search for an 'I' that is anterior to name; gender; action; fashion; matter itself.

It is important to recognise that those suffering from eating disorders often carry the added burden of stigmatising attitudes from the lay public and the medical profession. Eating disorders and their sufferers are commonly looked down upon as being preoccupied with superficial issues. In fact, anorexia can be a complex way of managing existential and spiritual crises. The theoretical contributions of philosophy and theology can help treat and encourage today's sufferers. Abnormal eating is not just a psycho-pathological phenomenon, but the coherent implementation of moral values with a long tradition in Western culture. Contrary to theorists who analyse the desire for thinness primarily as a response to contemporary popular culture, thinness does not have much to do with what we believe to be nice or beautiful – it is not simply a matter of what we find *pretty*. It is a matter of what we believe to be *good* and *right*. Eating disorders are not just the symptoms of an underlying mental disorder, as is often argued. They are the symptoms of extraordinary morality, which is being taken seriously – or more seriously than usual.

Thanks and acknowledgements

I am grateful to Gwen Davies, to the sponsors and students at Aberystwyth University, and everyone at New Welsh Review. I have also received kind support and encouragement from my family. I would like especially to thank James Sweetman, Benjamin Schaper, Duncan Driver and Holly Mak for their thoughtful comments about my early drafts. The staff of the English Department at the Chinese International School, with whom I worked while I was writing, were all invaluable mentors, as was Dr Sing Lee. Finally, I'm deeply grateful to my fiance, Adam Wessilinoff, for everything he is and does, and for being part of a happy new beginning.

About the Author

Catherine Haines was born in 1988 in Canberra, Australia and is a dual British-Australian citizen. In her final year of high school, she performed with the Shakespeare Globe Centre, and was awarded a National Achievement Scholarship by the Australian National University, from where she graduated with first class Double Honours in English and Philosophy and received commendation as top-ranked student in the School of Arts. In 2008, Catherine was awarded a Vice-Chancellor's Travel Grant to complete an acting diploma at the Royal Academy of Dramatic Art in London. Catherine went on to work as an actress and model while studying a Masters in English Literature at the University of Oxford. In 2013 Catherine moved to Hong Kong, where she was employed as an actress and a High School English teacher while completing a Certificate in Higher Education in Creative Writing at the University of Oxford. She is the winner of the New Welsh Writing Awards 2017 Aberystwyth University Prize for Memoir. In 2017, Catherine returned to Australia, where she is currently a PhD candidate at The University of Sydney.

CATEGORY WINNER, NEW WELSH WRITING AWARDS 2017
Available in print & ebook formats, £7.99

'Cath Barton writes her story... with such confidence and in prose that is so delightful to read, that I just couldn't put it down. It's beautiful. A delicate paean for coming together, full of understanding for the quirks and pitfalls and ultimate goodness in human nature.'

Mavis Cheek

WINNER OF THE NEW WELSH WRITING AWARDS 2016

Available in print & ebook formats

'Triumphs, in its lean prose and true dialogue… disarming humour & evocation of a family divided by sexism & racism. Stitches together threads of memory to create a moving tapestry of lost life, building bridges of understanding across time and place, enhancing literature's ever-changing, ever-supple genre.'

Rory MacLean

'Mandy Sutter's Nigeria rises like a mirage [creating] a complete arc of innovative concision.'

New Welsh Review

'Atmospheric wonderfully unexpected disquieting, touching and darkly humorous.'

Alison Moore

'We discern, in a microcosm, what has happened and is happening in macrocosm in much of the developing world.'

Penelope Shuttle